will there really be a morning?

Life: A Guide

Poems for Key Stage 2 with teaching notes

Compiled and introduced by
Fred Sedgwick

David Fulton Publishers

London

David Fulton Publishers Ltd
Ormond House, 26–27 Boswell Street, London WC1N 3JZ

www.fultonpublishers.co.uk

First published in Great Britain in 2002 by David Fulton Publishers

British Library Cataloguing in Publication Data

A catalogue record of this book is available from the British Library.

ISBN 1–85346–806–1

Typeset by FiSH Books, London
Printed and bound in Great Britain by Bell & Bain Ltd, Glasgow

Contents

Acknowledgements

The publishers would like to thank the following copyright holders for permission to use their material:

Sheena Billet, for her music for 'Lord of All Gardens', published here for the first time. Reproduced by permission of the composer.

John Cotton, for 'Listen', first published in *The Crystal Zoo* (Oxford University Press) and for 'Quiet', first published in *The Ammonite's Revenge*, with Fred Sedgwick (Tricky Sam! Enterprises). Reproduced by permission of the author.

Peter Dixon, for 'Auntie Win' and 'I am', published here for the first time. Reproduced by permission of the author.

John Gohorry, for 'Boredom', published here for the first time, and for 'I met an old man by the sea', first published in *This Way, That Way*, edited by Fred Sedgwick (Mary Glasgow). Reproduced by permission of the author.

John Mole, for 'Carnival Song', and 'She heard them shouting', from *The Dummy's Dilemma* (Hodder & Stoughton 1999). Reproduced by permission of the author.

Fred Sedgwick, for 'Stone', first published in *Smiths Knoll Magazine*, 23, 2000, and 'Lord of all gardens', published here for the first time. Reproduced by permission of the author.

Angela Topping, for 'The Creation Disco' and 'My Best Friend', published here for the first time. Reproduced by permission of the author.

Harvard University Press, for 'With Flowers', 'I'm Nobody' and 'Will There Really Be a Morning'. Reprinted by permission of the publishers and the Trustees of Amherst College from THE POEMS OF EMILY DICKINSON, Thomas H. Johnson, ed., Cambridge, Mass.: The Belknap Press of Harvard University Press, Copyright © 1951, 1955, 1979 by the President and Fellows of Harvard College.

Introduction

I first thought of this book as a collection of poems about feelings and emotions. I think we (my publisher and I) assumed that it would contain lots of words like 'affection', 'hatred', 'love', 'suffering', 'profound', 'heart-felt', 'passionate', 'envy' – as well as 'feelings' and 'emotions' themselves.

But we were wrong. Poems that tell the reader about how the writer feels about something are mostly boring. The function of poetry is not, as is conventionally supposed, to express the writer's feelings. The joys of self-expression, for the reader if not the self-indulgent writer, were a delusion of the 1960s, and should be dumped with the kaftans, the flares and (for my really old readers) the Donovan LPs. The function of poetry is twofold. Firstly, it exists to help the writer (and the reader) learn: poetry is the great teacher. And secondly, poetry exists to give pleasure. Somewhere Samuel Johnson sums this up (as he does so much else): 'The function of poetry is to help us enjoy and endure'.

While I was worrying about this book, I re-read the ending of Ernest Hemingway's novel *A Farewell to Arms*. The hero, a soldier, has just rushed back from the front to see his mistress, who is about to give birth. But, on his arrival, she is dead. The story ends like this: 'It was like saying goodbye to a statue. After a while I went out and left the hospital and walked back to the hotel in the rain'. I learnt again the power of understatement. How much more effective that passage is than this one, with which a bad writer might have finished his novel: 'I couldn't stand the pain of looking at her. It was as though there was a great grey stone in my head. My tears poured down my face in rivers as I ran through the corridors, startling nurses as I...' and so on, and so on. I don't want to know, I want to shout when a writer tells me what s/he feels. I want to know what it was like. Tell me the facts. The overt expression of feelings and emotions would have destroyed Hemingway's two terse sentences which, paradoxically, are full of feeling even though – I would say because! – they don't mention it. I was reminded of D.H. Lawrence's poem 'To Women, as Far as I'm Concerned': 'If people say they have got feelings, you may be pretty sure they haven't got them'.

And I began to see (I hope you don't mind if I make this personal) that if I am to understand your feelings and emotions, I don't need sentences beginning 'I feel..'. I need to know the facts, and I need to know the words you will choose to express your relationship to those facts. Poetry is not an expression of your personality, but an 'escape from it' (T. S. Eliot). I need to see the results of 'the intolerable struggle between words and meanings' (Eliot again). And that is true of the poets I read. It is especially true of the poets that I have included in this book.

Look, for example, at John Mole's poem 'She heard them shouting' (p. 20). Mole tells us nothing explicitly about the child's feelings. He tells a terrible truth: 'She heard them shouting . . .'. I suggest you re-do the poem in your mind with lots of conventional 'feeling' words in it, and see what it is like: it will be baggy, infinitely less emotional and thoroughly embarrassing. The child's terror comes across through the facts, and the understated way Mole uses them. He knows what all writers have to learn: that you can bring a tree down by undermining it. You don't have to blow it up.

Or look at the similar way in which Wes Magee builds the tension in 'Tracey's Tree' (p. 25). This poem is about a heart-breaking reality that almost every teacher has known at one time or another, the death of a child. There are no screeching brakes, and even the tears are 'only' rain, as they are in Hemingway's words. As Peter Dixon knows, it is the facts of a dead person's life – cushions, bus pass and, most movingly, 'a book mark/for Tomorrow/half way through the Psalms' (p. 36) that go on haunting us. 'Tracey's Tree' tells us all we need to know about the head teacher's feelings about the girl. Novelists say that you should not tell us what a character is like; you should show us. Perhaps that sums up the point I am labouring here.

Another idea I had at the beginning of this project was that the book should consist of poems about things that mattered. Unlike the explicit description of emotions, this idea stayed alive. Love, death, friendship, loneliness, anger, fear, the hills and the valleys, the flowers and the stars. This book is in part a reaction against other anthologies compiled for children. There is a kind of book that is typically like this (I have put in brackets the reasons for each dubious feature). It is a small collection (children can't cope with very much material in one book). It is printed on poor quality paper (children, unlike adults, don't need the best: whatever is cheap and available will do). It has scratchy cartoon-style illustrations, emphasising big noses and silly bottoms (children love 'zany' humour). And the poems are 'subversive' – Don't brothers have smelly socks? Aren't sisters soppy? Isn't school a bore? – (children like to see the mickey taken).

Since that unimaginable moment when the first two human babies became toddlers, children have run around chanting subversive verses about their parents and other adults. Well, I hope they have. Those chants have been about both life's trivia, and also about life's ferocious enormities, the big guns of the poet's armoury: love, death and sex. I have been collecting such rhymes for over 30 years. Because children chant verses like this in their playgrounds, there is no need for adults to write 'rude poems' for them. Such things are patronising. There is no need for Bimple on my Pottom poems, or Nogies up my Bose poems. Poems about Vartians Stealing my Mest are not wanted on voyage. (I hope my readers are familiar with Dr Spooner.) Children make such poems up anyway, thank God, and they do it better than we adults can. Nevertheless, the few publishers who produce poetry for children behave as though such work is what children will buy; that anything more demanding won't sell, because it will bore or distress children.

Most adults in the West find poetry embarrassing, or twee, or phoney in some way. I know this because even the most famous poets in Britain and the USA sell fewer copies of their books than the average successful novelists do. On the other hand, children love it. I know this as well, because I recite and read poetry to children almost every day of my working life. As soon as the rhythm, rhyme, good humour and sheer honesty of a fine poem becomes clear to a group of children, they settle down to listen and enjoy. Sometimes I come across evidence of even deeper enjoyment: a 10-year-old in Hendon said Thomas Hood's 'I Remember' (p. 38) along with me as I read it. She told me later that her parents were 'too busy' to read her poetry, but she had 'a pile of poetry books' by her bed. (Later she said something lovely to me as I walked to my car, one poetry reader to another: 'Will I ever see you again?')

I have made a book of poems that are about the central themes of what it is to be a human being. Religion is one theme, especially religious accounts of the creation, because we are all potentially creative artists. Indeed, as the collection grew, I found that it was becoming increasingly relevant to the teaching of religious education. The Old Testament seems to speak for humanity in all its conditions, especially in Ecclesiastes and the Psalms. But the collection became a book concerned with morality: how we get on, or don't get on, with each other. How we feel when we are alone. Lonely voices finding their way home speak in these poems. We can hear the eternal voice of unrequited love, every bit as sad when spoken by the Pueblo Indians as it is when spoken by a Western poet.

Another theme is the destruction of the world we live in. A quiet desperation is audible in John Cotton's poem about the environment, and Edward Thomas speaks to us about the poor who are always with us, and whom we mostly ignore. Neither of these poets preaches. Childhood, babyhood. Celebration. Time. Death. Fear. Questions. Mystery. That's the book I have made. I hope that it breaks down barriers between different curriculum subjects and themes, and that it is specially useful for Religious Education and Personal, Social and Moral Education.

In PSME, a central thread is how we can teach each other to face realities, and how we can accept that facing up to anything is never easy, never something in which we can train each other. It is never a skill: it is an act of courage. In teaching, facing up is central, because to teach is, etymologically, to show. Thus, if we want children to live lives that are moral, concealment can have no part in our teaching. And poetry is about truth. Wendy Cope, a poet who does reach the best-seller lists, said on Radio 4 recently: 'When a poem doesn't work, the first question to ask is "Am I telling the truth?"'

Many modern anthologies of poetry for children only include new work. I wanted this book to include a range of poetry from earlier centuries, because to be educated is, in part, to feel kinship with our ancestors as well as our contemporaries. We can hear children from two or three hundred years ago chanting in 'In and out the windows'. We can taste old jokes in 'Solomon Grundy', 'Be Merry' and 'I Saw'. We can sense the terror of the unknown in 'Meet-on-the-Road' and 'A Man of Words'. When the words of the Old Testament meet the translators of the King James Bible, we read sentences that are indisputably great. I feel that sparks fly between these pieces and new commissioned work. And the sparks fly again, today and for eternity, between all these poems and children.

With Flowers

I've nothing else – to bring, You know –
So I keep bringing These –
Just as the Night keeps fetching Stars
To our familiar eyes –

Maybe we shouldn't mind them –
Unless they didn't come –
Then – maybe, it would puzzle us
To find our way Home –

Emily Dickinson

Seven Wishes

Why can't I be the band that ties your forehead,
so close to your thoughts?

Why can't I be the nub of sweetcorn
you shred with your wildcat's teeth?

Why can't I be the turquoise round your neck
warmed by the storm of your blood?

Why can't I be the thread of many colours
that slides through your fingers on the loom?

Why can't I be the velvet tunic
over the ebb and flow of your heart?

Why can't I be the sand in your moccasins
that dares to stroke your toes?

Why can't I be your night's dream
when you moan in the black arms of sleep?

Pueblo Indians of New Mexico

The Creation Disco

First there was nothing
Then rain said 'let there be spring'.
And there was spring.

In the green wet grass
Where nothing had been but blades
Some crocus bubbled.

The daffodils and bluebells
Joined the party. And snakeshead fritillaries
Bent their spotted heads.

The spring disco-danced
All over the sprouting garden
In her best frock.

The party went on until
They were all worn out. The sun said
'Let there be summer'.

And there was.

Angela Topping

Listen

Silence is when you can hear things.
Listen:
The breathing of bees,
A moth's footfall,
Or the mist easing its way
Across the field,
The light shifting at dawn
Or the stars clicking into place
At evening.

John Cotton

Quiet

Once there was quiet in the valley,
We could hear the slow thoughts of mountains,
The breathing of small hills
And at evening the dark forest trees listening to the silence.
Then came traffic
And it was never the same.
The earth stopped hearing
And the still small voices were drowned.
Though sometimes in the small hours
The quiet will pay its sly secret visits
From where it waits.

John Cotton

The Owl

Downhill I came, hungry, and yet not starved;
Cold, yet had heat within me that was proof
Against the North wind; tired, yet so that rest
Had seemed the sweetest thing under the roof.

Then at the inn I had food, fire and rest,
Knowing how hungry, cold and tired was I.
All of the night was quite barred out except
An owl's cry, a most melancholy cry

Shaken out long and clear upon the hill,
No merry note, nor cause of merriment,
But telling me plain what I escaped
And others could not, that night, as in I went.

And salted was my food, and my repose,
Salted and sobered, too, by the bird's voice
Speaking for all who lay under the stars,
Soldiers and poor, unable to rejoice.

Edward Thomas

Lullaby Jazz for Daniel

Sleep little baby
in your wooden cot.
Your mother's gone out
but your father has not.
He's reading a book
by the flickering grate
and your mother has promised
she won't be late.

Sleep little baby.
God ensures
the planets are turning
beyond the trees.
To outer space
your worries have flown
and your father reads poems
all alone.

Sleep little baby
in your wooden cot.
Your mother's gone out
but your father has not.
He reads, folded up
in the big armchair,
then climbs to your room
to stroke your hair.

Sleep little baby.
Only God knows
what story under
your temples flows.
Dad's reading a book
by the flickering grate
and your mother has promised
she won't be late.

Fred Sedgwick

Carnival Song

Hoisted higher than us all
On your daddy's shoulders, girl.

Here is a world to see,
Here is your community.

Look out, look down,
Cry big love, spread it around.

Make it so we laugh with you,
Make old sadness pack and go.

This is everybody's street,
These are tomorrow's dancing feet.

All the colours, every skin,
A whole new life to be dressed in.

On your daddy's shoulders, girl, ride high,
Apple of our future's eye.

John Mole

I do not like thee, Doctor Fell

I do not like thee, Doctor Fell,
The reason why I cannot tell;
But this I know, I know full well,
I do not like thee, Doctor Fell.

Martial 1:32
(translated by Thomas Brown)

My Best Friend

We stand on the riverbank
while he shows me
where trout lie.

He knows the names
of all wild things
in the earth and sky.

He taught me colours
and animal prints,
bought me a kite.

We laugh a lot.
He tells old jokes
to make things right.

We play cards for money –
old pennies he's saved.
He's my best mate.

He buys me chips
in a drippy vinegar bag.
My grandad's great.

Angela Topping

I'm Nobody

I'm Nobody! Who are you?
Are you – Nobody – Too?
Then there's a pair of us!
Don't tell! They'd *advertise* – you know!

How dreary – to be – Somebody!
How public – like a Frog –
To tell *one's* name – the livelong June –
To an admiring Bog!

Emily Dickinson

I met an old man by the sea

I met an old man by the sea,
his beard was long and grey;
his coat was torn, his face was worn,
but still he stopped to play.

We played charades and I-spy,
Hopscotch and Drop-Down-Dead;
I asked him when his birthday was,
and this is what he said: –

'Tuesday the last of Never,
Wednesday the first of When,
Thursday the third of So-I've-heard;
clap hands and ask again!'

We played at Forfeits, Hunt-the-Fish,
Knock-knock and Guess-the-Word;
I asked his birthday once again
and this was what I heard: –

'Sunday the first of Sometimes,
Monday the last of What?
Friday the twelfth of Suit Yourself,
Saturday Mark-the-Spot.'

I asked his birthday one last time;
he rose, and shook his beard;
and this was what he said to me
before he disappeared: –

'Wednesday the ninth of Nothing,
Friday the fifth of Some;
Tuesday the last of Time-was-Past,
Time-Is and Time-to-Come.'

John Gohorry

Boredom

Nothing happens. Nothing happens all day.
The sky, the sky is a dull shade of grey.
I'm like a grey rock that rests on a grey stone,
undistinguished, an unrelieved grey monotone.

My heart's without music. What beats there?
As boring a beat as you'll find anywhere.
In the mind, nothing. Not a thought in my head.
Whatever you say, I just can't get interested.

Thanks all the same, but I'm too bored to argue.
Perhaps I should go back to sleep until tomorrow.
I write down my thoughts as they are occurring.
Odd, that rhyme happens. Rhyme must be boring.

Nothing happens. Nothing happens all day.
Each verse is the same dull shade of grey.

John Gohorry

Stone

It's a cool weight
in the palm of my hand.

It smells of pink earthworms coiled
on rainy mornings.

Hurled through the air,
it would hurt me badly.

If I tasted it,
it would taste of earth.

That wouldn't be so bad, perhaps,
to taste the earth.

Fred Sedgwick

In and out the windows

In and out the windows,
In and out the windows,
In and out the windows,
As you have done before.

Stand and face your lover,
Stand and face your lover,
Stand and face your lover,
As you have done before.

Follow her to London,
Follow her to London,
Follow her to London,
As you have done before.

Shake hands before you leave her,
Shake hands before you leave her,
Shake hands before you leave her,
As you have done before.

Traditional

She Heard Them Shouting

She heard them shouting at each other
Through her bedroom wall
But that was how it often was,
Nothing unusual.

She could never make out their words
Or begin to guess
Exactly what it was this time
Might have started the mess.

Once she lay awake
The whole night through,
Wondering what if anything
She could do.

Were they alseep yet,
Would it start again,
Would it be even louder
Or just the same?

She'd heard them shouting at each other
Through her bedroom wall
And now this silent waiting
Was worst of all.

John Mole

Life Is a Jest

Life is a jest; and all things show it,
I thought so once; but now I know it.

John Gay

When That I Was

When that I was and a little tiny boy,
  With hey, ho, the wind and the rain;
A foolish thing was but a toy,
  For the rain it raineth every day.

But when I came to man's estate,
  With hey, ho, the wind and the rain;
'Gainst knaves and thieves men shut their gates,
  For the rain it raineth every day.

But when I came, alas! to wive,
  With hey, ho, the wind and the rain;
By swaggering could I never thrive,
  For the rain it raineth every day.

But when I came unto my beds,
  With hey, ho, the wind and the rain;
With toss-pots still had drunken heads,
  For the rain it raineth every day.

A great while ago the world began,
  With hey, ho, the wind and the rain;
But that's all one, our play is done,
  And we'll strive to please you every day.

William Shakespeare (from *Twelfth Night*)

To Every Thing

To every thing there is a season,
and a time to every purpose under the heaven:

A time to be born, and a time to die;
a time to plant, and a time to pluck up that which is planted;

A time to kill, and a time to heal;
a time to break down, and a time to build up;

A time to weep, and a time to laugh;
a time to mourn, and a time to dance;

A time to cast away stones, and a time to gather stones together;
a time to embrace, and a time to refrain from embracing;

A time to get, and a time to lose;
a time to keep, and a time to cast away;

A time to rend, and a time to sew;
a time to keep silence, and a time to speak;

A time to love, and a time to hate;
a time of war, and a time of peace.

Ecclesiastes 3: 1–8

Solomon Grundy

Solomon Grundy,
Born on Monday,
Christened on Tuesday,
Married on Wednesday,
Took ill on Thursday,
Worse on Friday,
Died on Saturday,
Buried on Sunday.
This is the end
Of Solomon Grundy.

Traditional

Tracey's Tree

Last year it was not there,
the sapling with purplish leaves
planted in our school grounds with care.
It's Tracey's tree, my friend who died,
and last year it was not there.

Tracey, the girl with long black hair
who, out playing one day, ran
across a main road for a dare.
The lorry struck her. Now a tree grows
and last year it was not there.

Through the classroom window I stare
and watch the sapling sway.
Soon its branches will stand bare.
It wears a forlorn and lonely look
and last year it was not there.

October's chill is in the air
and cold rain distorts my view.
I feel a sadness that's hard to bear.
The tree blurs, as if I've been crying
and last year it was not there.

Wes Magee

Auntie Win
(a favourite aunt)

It's the dented cushions
and the half finished things that get you –
bits put aside for tomorrow...
   unwrapped sweets and parcels,
   bus pass in the purse,
   coins and pens and papers,
   pension book, and stamps...
      Her Bible, worn and broken,
      her chair with empty arms,
      a book mark
      for Tomorrow
         half way through the Psalms.

Peter Dixon

Be Merry

Whenever you see the hearse go by
And think to yourself that you're gonna die,
Be merry my friends, be merry.

They put you in a big white shirt
And cover you up with tons of dirt,
Be merry my friends, be merry.

They put you in a long-shaped box
And cover you over with tons of rocks,
Be merry my friends, be merry.

The worms crawl in and the worms crawl out,
They crawl in thin and they crawl out stout,
Be merry my friends, be merry.

Your eyes fall in and your hair falls out
And your brains come tumbling down your snout,
Be merry my friends, be merry.

Traditional

A Man of Words

A man of words and not of deeds
Is like a garden full of weeds;

And when the weeds begin to grow,
It's like a garden full of snow;

And when the snow begins to fall,
It is like birds upon a wall;

And when the birds begin to fly,
It's like a shipwreck in the sky;

And when the sky begins to roar,
It's like a lion at the door;

And when the door begins to crack,
It's like a stick across your back;

And when your back begins to smart,
It's like a penknife in your heart;

And when your heart begins to bleed,
You're dead, and dead, and dead indeed!

Traditional

The Hairy Toe

Once there was a woman who went out to pick beans
and she found a hairy toe.
She took the toe home with her
and that night, when she went to bed
the wind began to moan and groan.
Away off in the distance
she seemed to hear a voice crying:
Who's got my hairy toe?
Where's my hairy toe?

The woman scrooched down under the covers
way down under the covers
and about that time
the wind appeared to hit the house,
smoosh!
And the old house creaked and cracked
like something was trying get in.
The voice had come nearer now
almost at the door
and it said:
Who's got my hairy toe?
Where's my hairy toe?

The woman scrooched further down
under the covers
and pulled them tight around her head.
The wind growled around the house
like some big animal
and rumbled over the chimney.
All at once she heard the door creak
and something slipped in
and began to creep over the floor.
The floor went creak, creak
at every step that thing took towards her bed.
The woman could almost feel it
bending over her head
and then in an awful voice it said:
Who's got my hairy toe?
Where's my hairy toe?

YOU' VE GOT IT!

Traditional

To the Moon

'What have you looked at, Moon,
　　In your time,
　Now long past your prime?'
'O, I have looked at, often looked at
　　Sweet, sublime,
Sore things, shudderful, night and noon
　　In my time.'

'What have you mused on, Moon,
　　In your day,
　So aloof, so far away?'
'O, I have mused on, often mused on
　　Growth, decay,
Nations alive, dead, mad, aswoon,
　　In my day!'

'Have you much wondered, Moon,
　　On your rounds,
　Self-wrapt, beyond Earth's bounds?'
'Yea, I have wondered, often wondered
　　At the sounds
Reaching me of the human tune
　　On my rounds.'

'What do you think of it, Moon,
　　As you go?
　Is Life much, or no?'
'O, I think of it, often think of it
　　As a show
God ought surely to shut up soon,
　　As I go.'

Thomas Hardy

Prayer

From ghoulies and ghosties
And long-leggedy beasties
And things that go bump in the night,

Good Lord deliver us.

Traditional

Meet-on-the-Road

'Now, where are you going child?'
  Said Meet-on-the-Road.
'To school, sir, to school, sir,'
  Said Child-as-she-Stood.

'What have you got in your bag, child?'
  Said Meet-on-the-Road.
'My dinner, sir, my dinner, sir,'
  Said Child-as-she-stood.

'What have you got for your dinner, child?'
  Said Meet-on-the-Road.
'Some brown bread and cheese, sir,'
  Said Child-as-she-stood.

'Oh, then, give me some, right now,'
  Said Meet-on-the-Road.
'I've little enough for myself, sir,'
  Said Child-as-she-stood.

'What have you got that coat on for?'
  Said Meet-on-the-Road.
'To keep the wind and chill from me, sir,'
  Said Child-as-she-stood.

'I wish the wind would blow through you,'
    Said Meet-on-the-Road.
'Oh, what a wish, what a wish!'
    Said Child-as-she-stood.

'What are those bells ringing for?'
    Said Meet-on-the-Road.
'To ring bad spirits home again, sir,'
    Said Child-as-she-stood.

'Oh then, I must be going, child!'
    Said Meet-on-the-Road.
'So fare you well, so fare you well, sir,'
    Said Child-as-she-stood.

Traditional

I Am

I am the finger pinched in the door
I am the wobble on the new bike
I am the shiver in the cold bath
the scare in the darkness
the slip on the stair.

I am the tangle caught in a comb
the lump in the custard
the stone in the shoe.

I am the lonely
the friend we forget
the kiss, never given
the things we regret.

Peter Dixon

What are Heavy?

What are heavy? Sea-sand and sorrow:
What are brief? To-day and to-morrow:
What are frail? Spring blossoms and youth:
What are deep? The ocean and truth.

Christina Rossetti

I Remember

I remember, I remember,
The house where I was born,
The little window where the sun
Came peeping in at morn;
He never came a wink too soon,
Nor brought too long a day;
But now, I often wish the night
Had borne my breath away!

I remember, I remember,
The roses, red and white,
The violets, and the lily-cups,
Those flowers made of light!
The lilacs where the robin built,
And where my brother set
The laburnum on his birthday, –
The tree is living yet!

I remember, I remember,
Where I was used to swing,
And thought the air must rush as fresh
To swallows on the wing;
My spirit flew in feathers then,
That is so heavy now,
And summer pools could hardly cool
The fever on my brow!

I remember, I remember,
The fir trees dark and high;
I used to think their slender tops
Were close against the sky:
It was a childish ignorance,
But now 'tis little joy
To know I'm farther off from heaven
Than when I was a boy.

Thomas Hood

Riddle

Ten thousand children beautiful of this my body bred,
Both sons and daughters finely dekt, I live and they are dead.
My sons were put to extreme death by such as loved them well.
My daughters died with extreme age, but where I cannot tell.

[Mother – tree; sons – fruit; daughters – leaves.]

Traditional

I Saw

I saw a peacock with a fiery tail
I saw a blazing comet drop down hail
I saw a cloud with ivy circled round
I saw a sturdy oak creep on the ground
I saw an ant swallow up a whale
I saw a raging sea brim full of ale
I saw a Venice glass sixteen foot deep
I saw a well full of men's tears that weep
I saw their eyes all in a flame of fire
I saw a house as big as the moon and higher
I saw the sun even in the midst of night
I saw the man that saw this wondrous sight.

Traditional

Now the Hungry Lion Roars

Now the hungry lion roars,
    And the wolf behowls the moon;
Whilst the heavy ploughman snores,
    All with weary task fordone.
Now the wasted brands do glow,
    Whilst the screech-owl, screeching loud,
Puts the wretch that lies in woe
    In remembrance of a shroud.
Now it is the time of night
    That the graves, all gaping wide,
Every one lets forth his sprite,
    In the church-way paths to glide:
And we fairies, that do run
    By the triple Hecate's team,
From the presence of the sun,
    Following darkness like a dream,
Now are frolic; not a mouse
Shall disturb this hallow'd house:
I am set with broom before,
To sweep the dust behind the door.

William Shakespeare
(from *A Midsummer Night's Dream*)

Goodnight

Here's a body – there's a bed!
There's a pillow – here's a head!
There's a curtain – here's a light!
There's a puff – and so good night!

Thomas Hood

Lord of All Gardens (Kyrielle)

for Rebecca Moore, on the occasion of her first Communion, 10 June 2001

The garden's soaked in sunlight where,
Marooned in my mortality,
I stand and murmur common prayer:
Lord of all gardens, pray for me.

Mysteriously float the scents
Of herb and flower, grass and tree.
The cat hunts slyly by the fence.
Lord of all gardens, pray for me.

Where the sky above me stands
Clouds' silent music's drifting free.
My mind is still. So are my hands.
Lord of all gardens, pray for me.

With the wide world, or all alone;
Whether in air, on land or sea,
My heart won't turn to sand or stone –
Lord of all gardens, pray for me.

Fred Sedgwick

Kyrielle

Psalm 23

The LORD is my shepherd; I shall not want.
He maketh me to lie down in green pastures:
he leadeth me beside the still waters.
He restoreth my soul:
he leadeth me in the paths of righteousness
for his name's sake.
Yea, though I walk through the valley of the shadow of death,
I will fear no evil: for thou art with me;
thy rod and thy staff they comfort me.
Thou preparest a table before me in the presence of mine enemies:
thou anointest my head with oil; my cup runneth over.
Surely goodness and mercy shall follow me
all the days of my life:
and I will dwell in the house of the LORD
for ever.

God Be in My Head

God be in my head,
And in my understanding;

God be in my eyes,
And in my looking;

God be in my mouth,
And in my speaking;

God be in my head,
And in my thinking;

God be at my end,
And at my departing.

Sarum Missal

Will There Really Be a 'Morning?'

Will there really be a 'Morning'?
Is there such a thing as 'Day'?
Could I see it from the mountains
If I were as tall as they?

Has it feet like water lilies?
Has it feathers like a bird?
Is it brought from famous countries
Of which I have never heard?

Oh some Scholar! Oh some Sailor!
Oh some Wise Men from the skies!
Please to tell a little Pilgrim
Where the place called 'Morning' lies!

Emily Dickinson

Teaching Notes

Teaching important subjects is difficult. Many teachers have traditionally avoided them. They have taught easy ones – Ourselves, People Who Help Us, the Vikings – subjects that are not, on the face of it, contentious. Now that teachers no longer choose what they teach, the National Curriculum encourages them to play safe. But this difficulty in teaching children about death and love and life – the very essences of Personal Social and Moral Education (PSME), of course, as well as what I have called the big guns in the poet's armoury – this difficulty, although obviously a problem, is the best reason for trying to do it. We should not be interested in a quiet life, but in the good life: the good life in the philosophical sense, a life that is examined, a life that is curious, a life that is lived by someone who pays attention to the search for truth. Whenever the controversial emerges in the classroom, the chance of real education increases. The temperature rises, and the pupils' and the teacher's engagement ensures learning. In Ted Hughes' phrase, we are working at 'top pressure'.

Of course there is risk. There is a risk of tears, for example, if the teacher teaches a poem about death when one of the children has just lost a grandma, or a parent, or even a pet. But much as all art involves a risk of distress (among, of course, many other things) it also risks a kind of joy. There is also a risk of controversy. No risk is seriously involved when we teach infants about the people who help us: the nurse, the policeman, the crossing patrol.

What follows are notes on some of the poems in this book, and how we might use the poems to get children writing. I mentioned the risk of tears above: there is also a risk of difficulty when we teach poetry about important subjects, and I hope that in these notes I have succeeded in suggesting ways to help children read poems. Close reading, with the senses alert for rhyme in all its variations, for rhythm, for the power of metaphor and simile, and for the sheer music of verse is the only way to make a poem ours. And when we make good poems ours, we grow mentally, psychologically and spiritually. We enrich our imagination, which in turn helps us to understand people who are different from ourselves, and yet linked to us by our common humanity.

But another, less widely recognised, way of coming to terms with these poems is to write in the grip of them. In other words, children should confront them in an active way and make their own poems. I have included in these notes some examples of children writing in classes that I have taught: I hope that they might be useful in tandem with the main part of the book.

Some advice applies to all reading of poetry, whether by adults or children: read slowly. Don't just see the words, don't just hear them: taste them. In other words, let the poem take its time with you, and even move your lips as you read it. When there is something difficult in a poem, slide over it the first time you read it, concentrating on the poem's music; and then return to it for a second, third, fourth, fifth reading and think about it. If it is a good poem, it will eventually become yours and you will read it hundreds of times, getting something new from it each time. If you have already made poems yours, you will know this. If you haven't – trust me.

The notes on the poems have one, two or three parts:

1.   A section on reading the poem, and helping the children to read it. I mean 'read' here in the sense of 'understand' and 'enjoy'. To read a poem well is to 'make it yours', and to teach it well is to help children to make it theirs.

2.   A section on helping the children to write in the grip of the poem.

3.   A section on performing the poem. Most of the poems suitable for performance are towards the end of the book.

With Flowers

Emily Dickinson

Emily Dickinson stands at the beginning to welcome the reader, her arms full of flowers and stars. Ask the children to read this poem to each other, moving their lips, tasting the words. Ask them: does this poem rhyme?

It half-rhymes: these/stars/eyes; them/come/home. The form of the poem – two neat four-line stanzas – looks complete enough. It promises a kind of simple satisfaction: here are two little neatly carpentered boxes. It looks like a nursery rhyme. But the rhymes, which are slant-rhyme, para-rhyme (other words for half-rhyme) deny that satisfaction. Don't be so sure, they seem to say ... It certainly isn't a nursery rhyme.

Can the children think of other para-rhymes? Look around the room. There is the door. 'Far' half-rhymes with 'door'. The 'wall'? 'Well'. Ask the children to find half-rhymes for 'sun', 'moon', 'grass', 'stone', 'chair', 'break'. Work out some for yourself beforehand. 'Fen', 'bane', 'dross', 'stain', 'flower' and 'creek' suggest themselves to me. Looking at my bookshelves, I think of 'word' and 'sword'; 'rhyme' and 'home' – both very suggestive pairs. Thinking in terms of half-rhymes releases a whole new set of electrical connections in a language that is notoriously poor in rhyme (relative to Russian, for example).

> I watch the evening sun
> Drop over the stagnant fen

One great exponent of half-rhyme was Wilfred Owen. Read the first four lines of his 'Strange Meeting', and ask the children to listen for half-rhymes:

> It seemed that out of battle I escaped
> Down some profound dull tunnel, long since scooped
> Through granites which titanic wars had groined.
> Yet also there encumbered sleepers groaned, ...

Emily Dickinson's poem is punctuated eccentrically. Ask the children to read the poem in pairs, pausing at the dashes. Ask them why certain nouns are capitalised.

Get the children to write a poem to give to a parent with another gift: 'With chocolates', for example; or to accompany a gift to a baby sister or brother: 'With a teddy bear'. Suggest a few opening lines:

> I bought this today...

> I found this today...

> I knew about you and sweets, so I...

I have made some notes for a poem:

> I found this poem in my garden yesterday.
> I'd been looking for another one
> all the day before, with lupins
> blaring like trombones, but I found this one
> with its mysterious scents, and its sly cat...

Ask the children to use half-rhymes, if they can. Do not insist on it.

Ask the children to write a poem beginning 'Finding our way home'. They could set it in many places:

In the snow (begin with footsteps. Don't forget the sound and feel of them, as well as their appearance).

In the fog.

In an aeroplane.

They might use half-rhyme; they might use dashes in their poems if they thought they felt right.

Seven Wishes

Pueblo Indians of

New Mexico

For reasons implicit in PSME, it is important for young people to hear and read the words of peoples different from themselves. In this poem, inheritors of an oral tradition on the other side of the Atlantic ask universal questions. Indeed, this is a poem made up entirely of questions. They form a love poem.

But children play brilliantly with other kinds of question. Ask them: 'Can you think of a question that you would love to know the answer to, but you don't think you ever will?'

When I do this, I impose silence and darkness on them for a minute – asking them to close their eyes and think of three such questions. The following questions came from a group of nursery children. When the questions were read back to them, they were asked to decide which was the most important one. That was used as a refrain in a poem:

Questions

Why do you get older when it's your birthday?
Why have people got names?
How do people talk
And how does the sun light up?

How does the river move?
Why are beaches by the sea?
Why are there millions of stones by the beach
And how does the sun light up?

How does chicken pox come?
Why do babies cry?
Why does Dad fight with Mum
And how does the sun light up?

How come wild animals are not in the street?
How does your heart get inside you?
Is God inside your body
And how does the sun light up?

Other questions I have collected over the years from children are:

How can I tell if a man is evil or not?

Does God believe in me?

Why do adults have power over children when children do not have power over grown-ups?

How do you get up to heaven?

Why does gravity hold you down?

Three Muslim children at the Islamic Centre, Stanmore, London composed the following philosophical poem based on important questions:

How Will the Day of Judgement Begin?

Will there ever be peace in the world?
When will life end?
How many animals are there in the world?
How will the Day of Judgement begin?

Will people from different religions go to heaven?
Is there such a thing as an immortal person?
How hot is the fire of hell?
How will the Day of Judgement begin?

Is there such a thing as luck?
Are there such things as ghosts?
Will Man ever be able to create a living thing?
When will Islam dominate?
How will the Day of Judgement begin?
                    Mahdi (10), Ali (10), Aunali (8)

I have collected questions from even younger children. We all hear questions like these from time to time. Writing them down bears fruit in later years. I have arranged this into lines:

How do we know the world began
with a big bang
when there weren't any scientists around –
not even dinosaur scientists?
                    Daniel (5)

The same child said to his mother, as she was dismantling the Silver Cross pram so that she could stow it away in the loft:

Are you putting that away
For when I'm a baby again?

Daniel (3)

When the children have played with questions in these ways,
they might look again at 'Seven Wishes', and read it in pairs.
Can they imagine liking someone so much that they would like
to be the 'sand in their moccasins'? What would be modern,
British equivalents of these questions?

Why can't I be

your computer's keys
so that you have to touch me
every day?

Why can't I be
the buttons on your tv
so you have to turn me
before you can watch anything?

Why can't I be
the spoon that stirs your tea,
the lock that takes your key,
the carpet on your stairs –
no, I don't mind
how worn I'd get to be.
Who cares?

Why can't I be
the sea you swim in,
the sea you allow to trickle
over your whole body,
that you allow, sometimes, to rage?
I'd take you gladly
from shore to shore to shore.

Why can't I be
your star –
the evening star or the pole star.
I'd guide you through the darkest nights.

I know.
It's too much to ask.

But
why can't I be
your computer's keys
so that you have to touch me
every day?

Fred Sedgwick

I have collected some questions from children using this poem, and arranged them in a class poem. Thanks to the children at Radburn School, Letchworth, Hertfordshire:

Why can't I be the puppy
You kiss on the head and stroke?
Why can't I be the bracelet on your perfect shaped arms?
Why can't I be the romantic book
That you read every night?
Why can't I be the helicopter
That saves you from a watery grave?
Why can't I be the clock that you put near you
When you go to sleep at night?
Why can't I be the angel
That whispers in your ear at night?
Why can't I be the nightlight
That shimmers on your desk at night?
Why can't I be the phone that waits impatiently for your
    voice?
Why can't I be the lolly that you lick?

This poem makes an excellent performance poem. Ask seven children to read one question each in an assembly about questions, or one about love. Suggest that they adopt the tone of a child asking 'Why can't I have an ice cream?'

The Creation Disco

Angela Topping

This poem can be taught alongside other creation accounts. One is Genesis 1:1–2:3, obviously:

In the beginning God created the heaven and the earth. And the earth was without form, and void: and darkness was upon the face of the deep. And the Spirit of God moved upon the face of the waters. And God said, Let there be light: and there was light. And God saw the light, that it was good: and God divided the light from the darkness. And God called the light Day, and the darkness he called Night. And the evening and the morning were the first day. And God said, Let there be a firmament in the midst of the waters, and let it divide the waters from the waters. And God made the firmament, and divided the waters which were under the firmament from the waters that were above the firmament: and it was so. And God called the firmament Heaven. And the evening and the morning were the second day.

And God said, Let the waters under the heaven be gathered together unto one place, and let the dry land appear: and it was so. And God called the dry land Earth; and the gathering together of the waters called he Seas: and God saw that it was good. . . .

And here is part of a Maori account. Io is the Supreme Being:

There was no glimmer of dawn, no clearness, no light.
Io began by saying these words:
'Darkness, become a light-possessing darkness'
And at once light appeared.
He said:
'Light, become a darkness-possessing light'
And an intense darkness came.
Then he spoke a third time:
'Let there be one darkness above,
Let there be one darkness below,
Let there be one light above,
Let there be one light below.'
And a great light prevailed.
And Io spoke a fourth time:
'Waters, be separate,
Heaven, be formed.'
The sky became suspended
And the moving earth lay stretched ahead.

A New Zealand Creation myth.
adapted from Ellen van Wolde, *Stories from the Beginning:
Genesis 1–11 and Other Creation Stories* (London: SCM
Press, 1999)

Here is a child writing her own creation myth:

One day God said 'I'm lonely. I will make something to keep
me company.' He made a dog but the dog looked sad.
'What's the matter?' Dog said, 'God I'm so lonely.'

So God made lots of dogs but they ate him out of house and
home. So he said 'I will make you a world and you can live
on it.' So he did. But there was not any light, or food, or
water. So God got some fire and rolled it into a ball and threw
it above the earth.

'I will call you Sun,' said God, feeling really pleased.

But then something very strange happened. Bits of the sun
kept falling off. It did not seem very pleased to be a ball in the
sky. God grabbed what was left of the sun and took it apart.
He put some clay in the middle of it and put it back in its
place and the little bits of the sun that had fallen off the sun
he called stars.

Then he sat on the edge of his garden with his legs dangling
down into space. He stamped on his world and made holes
in it. He went into a well and got water and put it into all the
little holes.

Just then God's friend Mountain came along, stamping and shaking salt all over the place. 'Don't do that!' said God. 'Now look what you have done!' Mountain looked at God's world. There were lumps in it and the water was salt. God sat down and said 'Dear oh dear I wish there were not vibrations. I don't see why you had to stamp, Mountain. And as for shaking salt, look what you have done to my sea!'

But the dogs had guessed that this might happen, so they had made tunnels in the earth, and some of the fresh water had run into them. Then the dogs had found some un-dry clay and made a cover for them and called them river, stream, lake and spring.

Meanwhile God had decided to call all the lumps mountains after his friend. The dogs said, 'We want food.' so God made some other kinds of creatures and things for them to eat, but they argued about their food, so God made a chart for everyone, like this:

COW–GRASS

Then the dogs went up to God. 'We want something to see and sleep on,' they said.

So God made plants, shrubs, trees and grass. Then he went to bed.

The next day he got up. The dogs came round him and pestered him all morning for something to play with. In the end God got cross. 'Be satisfied,' he said. So they went away from a very tired God.

He went straight to bed and the dogs made a plan. They got all of God's clay and got in a long line. One by one they solemnly got some clay, threw it into the sky and named it.

There was Mars, Saturn and a lot of others. Then God woke up. He decided to make the dogs something to do. He got his bag with clay in it. There was only a little bit. God knew at once it was the dogs, so he made them two things to make them work as a punishment. He called them humans. Then he ran out of clay.

Well, at least it gave the dogs something to do, and God was satisfied.

Vashti (9)
(Camps Hill School, Stevenage, 1969)

Or, more briefly, children might write a spring disco, or a Christmas disco, or a holiday disco, each one using Angela Topping's first line 'First there was nothing...'

Two poems by John Cotton

Here is a chance to examine two little poems in free verse by the same poet. 'Listen' is beautifully made up of a list of things that can't really be heard at all – at least, not without a superhuman effort. Among others, what notable technique does John Cotton use in 'Quiet'? This is a chance to explain personification: the mountains, hills, and trees are represented as persons, or possibly animals, that think, breathe and listen.

Listen

John Cotton

This is so simple to teach effectively. As John Cotton himself has suggested, sit in the silence for a while. I would add 'close your eyes'. Then ask the children to make 'listen' poems, perhaps stealing (John Cotton won't mind) the first two lines of his poem.

When I do this, I start with sounds 'in your body'. Then I move to sounds 'in the classroom'. Then, 'in the next room... outside... can you imagine sounds from outer space, or under the sea...'.

Or you can put in the poem, as Cotton does, sounds you'd like to hear, but can't: 'the flick of a blackbird's tail at the end of the lawn...'.

It is worth noting that, although this poem is unrhymed, the chiming of the 'ing' syllables through its short length sound a little bell-like music.

Some children at Radburn School wrote:

Listen
I heard
A whistling sound
Like the whispering
Of the wind.
I heard
The scraping of chairs
Like a witch's toe
Scratching the ground.
I can hear
The computer
Like a very quiet
Hair dryer.
I would like to hear
The sound of dandelions
Singing in the sun.
I would like to hear
Great Grandma speak again
Because there are
A couple of things
I would like to tell her.

It is easy to write poems about the environment and the decline in its quality that are preachy. This poem is subtle and does its job more effectively for not telling us what to think.

Work with this poem as with the previous one, but in the open air.

Quiet
John Cotton

This is a good poem for discussion. Give the children a photocopy of it, and read it as clearly as you can. Point especially at the line 'Speaking for all who lay under the stars'. Who are they? Discuss with the children tramps, the homeless and refugees. Get them to write a poem that speaks for them.

These lines from *King Lear* might help in this context:

> Poor Tom; that eats the swimming frog; the toad, the tadpole, the wall-newt, and the water; that in the fury of his heart, when the foul fiend rages, eats cow-dung for sallets; swallows the old rat and the ditch-dog; drinks the green mantle of the standing pool; who is whipped from tithing to tithing, and stock-punished, and imprisoned; who hath three suits to his back, six shirts to his body . . .

Show the children that the early part of Edward Thomas' poem is built on threes: 'hungry . . . cold . . . tired; . . . food, fire and rest'. There is a good reason for this: there are always three caskets, three billy goats Gruff to trip-trap over the troll's bridge, three bears whose porridge was eaten, chairs sat in and beds slept in. Three is a magic number: two and four are always less satisfying. Show the children that the owl's cry seems even longer than Thomas describes it, because of the line and stanza break between 'cry' and 'Shaken'. Show them, too, that the poem begins with the poet's ease ('Downhill I came') contrasting with the 'Soldiers and poor'.

The Owl
Edward Thomas

Can the children remember any lullabies from their own young childhood?

> Matthew, Mark, Luke and John
> Bless the bed that I lie on.
> Four corners to my bed,
> Four angels round my head,
> 　　One to watch
> 　　And one to pray
> And two to bear my soul away.

Lullaby Jazz for Daniel
Fred Sedgwick

This last line is altered in a modern anthology to: 'And two to keep me safe alway'. The children might usefully discuss why this change has been made, and whether they think it was a good or bad change.

Or do they know any poems about going to bed?

This is a little anonymous poem:

> There is no need to light a night-light
> On a night like tonight;
> For a night-light's light's a slight light
> When the moonlight's white and bright.

Ask the children to write a lullaby for a baby brother or sister, or for a pet, or for a grandparent. It might be a good idea to collect from the children words with soft lulling sounds in them: few lullabies will work if they are filled with letters like 'b', 'd' and 'k'.

Or what might be a good challenge – write a violent lullaby:

Lullaby for a Child Giant

Bang yourself to bye-byes
   you great brute.
Close your bloodshot eyes.
   Quickly! Shoot

your thinking dead and
   divert it into dreams
where everything is not quite
   what it seems.

Bash your bison brain
   and blunderbuss
yourself into deep silence
   and don't bother us.

And when you wake tomorrow
   we will cast
nets for a shark for you
   to break your fast.

Fred Sedgwick

Carnival Song

John Mole

Here is a picture of a carnival in England where people of 'every skin' are celebrated. The children should look at the rhymes in this poem. Are they full rhymes or half-rhymes, as in Emily Dickinson's poem at the beginning of this collection?

Could the children collect pictures of carnivals, and pick out one figure to write a poem about?

Ask the children to make up a name that is easy to rhyme with. Here are some common English rhyme sounds:

oo (with variants like u, ough), ee, (ea, etc), ow, an, al, at, ot, in

and write a poem like this one:

> I do not like you, Albie Mann.
> I dislike you all I can.
> I am not your biggest fan.
> I do not like you, Albie Mann.
>
> I do not like you, Janie True.
> I'd like to flush you down the loo.
> I do not like you or your crew.
> I do not like you through and through.

...and then make a four-line verse like this one. It might be easier for the children to do this exercise in groups of four or five.

Here is the original Latin. Surprising as it may seem, children love short bursts of a foreign language. I get them to say it after me, and then the whole poem together in one of the English translations. The man Martial dislikes, without knowing why, is Sabidius:

> Non amo te, Sabidi, nec possum dicere quare:
> Hoc tantum posse dicere, non amo te.

I Do Not Like Thee, Doctor Fell
Martial

I have often used Angela Topping's poem with children. I show it to them and ask them to write about a best friend, leaving a surprise to the end. I ask them to write in short lines, as Angela Topping does. They should try to feel where each line should end. Or they could write in words of a certain number of words or syllables. But it often works if you simply say: Write in short lines, because poets are paid by the line...'

> My best friend
> taught me
> how to say Dad and cow
> in African.
> We do things together

My Best Friend
Angela Topping

like play board games
like Monopoly.
She buys me earrings
and when she went to Africa
she brought me back
a necklace made of wood and cow.
She taught me how
to flip a pancake
without
dropping it on the floor.
I love my Aunty.

Sophie (9)

He stands with me in the
Dark while we watch bats
Fly about in the sky.
We go on holiday.
We visit crabs that
Crawl about, and sea
Shells and sand.
He says he loves me.
I love him. He
Buys me toys
Like millennium bug.
He taught me
The types of snakes
Like side winder
And grass snake.
He stops me getting hurt.
I love my brother.

Shane (8)

An exercise in rhyme

Angela Topping's poem rhymes, of course. Ask the children to
identify the rhymes. Give the children certain words, and ask
them to find rhymes for them. This time they are looking for
full rhymes. Make sure that they understand that 'm' words do
not rhyme with 'n' rhymes – a common mistake. 'Room', for
example, does not rhyme with 'soon'.

I met an old man by the sea
John Gohorry

Young children love this poem. It needs to be read in a jaunty,
snappy way. You need to emphasise the rhythmic differences
between the stanzas in italics and the stanzas in Roman type.
Children love the nonsense parts ('first of Sometimes' etc): I
think they are especially effective because of the cage of
metrical correctness that surrounds them.

I'm Nobody!

Emily Dickinson

Ask the children to read this poem carefully, and also to re-read 'With Flowers'. Ask them: what is the difference between the rhymes in the two poems? This poem, of course, has full rhymes, including the clumping, dismissive 'Frog/Bog!' The last word, with its capital letter, its exclamation mark (printers used to call these 'screamers'), and with that hefty rhyme, almost demands to be shouted.

Ask the children again: do you ever feel that you are nobody? Loneliness is something we have to deal with in the PSME curriculum. Note, however, that Dickinson doesn't regret being alone. Write a poem beginning with that title. It could be sad – or it could be glad.

Boredom

John Gohorry

It must be a difficult and risky thing to write a poem about boredom that is not itself boring. But John Gohorry has achieved it. What does he do to make his poem smell and taste, as it were, of boredom? Ask the children to count the number of words that are repeated, and write them down. Repetition often equals boredom. Ask them to count all the words that we associate with dullness. I count 'nothing', 'dull' itself, 'grey', 'monotone', all words beginning with 'un-', and 'boring'. Somehow, also, the flat rhythms of the poem describe boredom in their movement.

Ask the children to write a poem beginning with John Gohorry's first line. Ask them to repeat words about dullness. Looking up 'dull' in a thesaurus would be one way to begin. Mine offers: 'flat', 'dead', 'slack', 'tame', 'limp', 'lifeless', 'colourless', 'pale' ... and many others.

Stone

Fred Sedgwick

Ask the children to find an ordinary object, and then to write about it with as many of the five senses as they can keep fully in mind. They will probably write vividly if you encourage them to draw the stone, or leaf, or twig, or brick or whatever, with great care, while looking at it (as William Blake put it) 'until it hurts'. For some suggestions on helping children to draw with intensity, see my book *Enabling Children's Learning through Drawing and Writing* (David Fulton 2002). These suggestions include:

Make the children explore various ways of making pencil marks.

Don't let them use erasers.

Ensure that they look while they are drawing.

Ensure that they think about scale: the drawing should be big enough to make the details clear.

63

In and Out the Windows

Traditional

This old rhyme offers a chance for some teaching about prepositions. I find that definitions of prepositions are unhelpful; but, like love, we know them when we come across them. Ask the children to play with prepositions, like 'in', 'out', 'before', 'behind', 'beneath', 'inside', 'under'. How many can they collect? Widen this to prepositional phrases: 'in front of', 'down behind,' 'over the top of' etc. Ask the children to write a stanza like the first stanza in this poem. Here is a poem written by a child. She has simply used prepositions and prepositional phrases, and they have set her free to write excellent lines.

> Behind the door
> And inside my head
> The blood rushes
> Like people running
> To catch a train
> In a far-off station
> Which is beyond the stars.
>
> Through my brain
> Rattle the days
> Of the past
> And the bad and the good.
> Over my mind
> Passes round the work
> That has to be done.
>
> Along the silent path
> That is secret
> There will be red roses
> That are prisoned
> In my brain.

Emma (10)

Suggested first lines:

> Down below the rafters
>
> In and out the garden

It seems to me that a long time has passed between the beginning of 'In and out the windows' and the end, and much has happened. Ask the children to think about this.

She Heard Them Shouting

John Mole

Here John Mole bravely addresses an essential subject in PSME. Marital discord is, of course, a delicate and dangerous one. Some might suggest that therefore we shouldn't tackle it in schools. I think the contrary is true: the delicate and dangerous subjects are the most important, and our teaching of them is the most educational teaching that we can do, because these subjects are the ones that matter. It is easy, as I have already written, to teach a topic to children about People Who Help Us, referring to the postman and the nurse and the school caretaker and so on. That is why teachers often do teach this topic. It doesn't help children – the thousands of them – who have been brought up in breaking homes, and all the other children who haven't, but who worry both about the possibility, and about the predicament that their friends are in. And, of course, even children in the happiest homes have cause to worry at times about dangerous, electric silences.

I would simply read this poem to children, leave a silence, and then read something cheerful to sweeten the palate. I think that children should have an opportunity to write poems inspired by this one. I don't think it would be difficult to do, either. But I don't see how, morally, we could as teachers justify the potential opening of windows that both we, the children and their parents might regret.

We might usefully help the children to notice how John Mole's near-repetition of the first stanza at the end of the poem suggests, sadly, that the shouting will go on and on; that soon, the next night, or the night after that, it will happen again. Repetition of key lines is something that children never do in their writing until the usefulness of it is pointed out to them; and it is demonstrated brilliantly here in John Mole's poem.

Life Is a Jest
John Gay

Life is a joke:

Ask the children to write out a funny thing that has happened to them. Can they reduce it to two lines of poetry? It doesn't have to rhyme.

When That I Was
William Shakespeare

I treat this as a performance poem. There are several more coming up. One way of teaching this song is to divide the children into two groups. One group has to say 'With hey, ho, the wind and the rain' when you point to it, and the other group has to say 'For the rain it raineth every day' when you point to *it*. In the meantime, you say all the other lines. I would include 'For the rain it raineth every day' at the end of the last verse too, where it doesn't appear in the Shakespeare, and then I would add his last line:

A great while ago, the world began,
    With hey, ho, the wind and the rain;
But that's all one, our play is done,
    For the rain it raineth every day
[LONG PAUSE]
    And we'll strive to please you every day.

Then, the children could take over the other lines from you.

It is not difficult to explain the slightly obscure references in this song: as a man I was a crook, a thief (verse 2); my wife wasn't impressed by my showing off (verse 3); I drank too much beer with my friends ('toss-pots') (verse 4).

In case there are any enthusiasts for settings of Shakespeare's songs, I recommend three recordings of this one. The first is by the extraordinary counter-tenor Alfred Deller, and you can find it on *Shakespeare's Songs* by the Deller Consort, on Harmonia Mundi. The second is by the tenor John Potter on *Songs and Dances from Shakespeare* by The Broadside Band, on Past Times. The third is an Irish-influenced setting. It is sung by Ben Kingsley, and is part of the soundtrack of Trevor Nunn's film of *Twelfth Night*. I am listening to Deller now as I write this. I am conscious of action by the hairs on the back of my neck. It entrances children too.

To Every Thing

Ecclesiastes

This is another performance poem. One child reads the introduction, the first two lines, and the other children read the rest of the contrasting verses in pairs. They should study the words carefully first. Some of the phrases demand being spoken in a rising intonation: the ones ending 'born', 'build up', 'laugh', 'dance', 'embrace', etc; and others demand being read with the voice dropping: 'die', obviously; 'kill'; weep' . . . and so on. This should help the children to appreciate not only the profundity of these lines, but also the balanced elegance of this translation, which comes from the King James Bible. The children could study other translations and compare them. Which do they prefer? I suggest they look at *The New International Version*, *The New English Bible* and the *Jerusalem Bible*.

I am writing these notes ten days after the terrorist atrocity in New York. Last week I used these words in a school and they had a resonance that was very moving. I did not try to explain any of them. Words like this should be left in the classroom with a silence after them.

On an infinitely more trivial note, could the children write a school version of these lines? Here is a suggested beginning:

A time to run, and a time to stop running . . .

Or a school year version:

A time for silence in September, and a time for noise at the Christmas disco . . .

A similar traditional piece goes, of course, like this:

Solomon Grundy

Traditional

Monday's child is fair of face,
Tuesday's child is full of grace,
Wednesday's child is full of woe,
Thursday's child has far to go,
Friday's child is loving and giving,
Saturday's child works hard for a living,
And the child that is born on the Sabbath day
Is bonny and blithe and good and gay.

Coach the children in performing the poem like this – one child speaks the first part of each line, and other children the rest:

Monday's child – fair of face,
Tuesday's child – full of grace,
Wednesday's child – full of woe,
Thursday's child – far to go,
Friday's child – loving and giving,
Saturday's child – works hard for a living
And the child that is born on the Sabbath day –
bonny and blithe and good and gay.

Ask the children to write weekly poems, or monthly ones, like this:

A Life

You were born in January, with the year as white
As the paper you're writing on, at dead of night.

You remembered your cradle and the wooden hood
Where the snow came drifting, as we knew it would.

You toddled in March on the windy sand
In nappies and knickers and anorak and

In April you hoped school would be OK
And the bustling bullies wouldn't come your way.

In May dressed up in a blazer, black,
You gazed like the moon at the railway track

Which took you in June to Dylan Street,
Holes in the soles of the shoes on your feet.

July – you'd found a passable way
To earn a living day by day.

Under foreign sun, in a sweltering town
You dawdled the little streets up and down.

In late September, at a football game
You chanted a boyish hero's name.

In October, at Colinsford Fair
You swung on a ship and a wing and a prayer.

November came as you pulled at your hood
By a bonfire crazed with flame and wood.

It's December, and the year's as white
As the paper you're writing on at dead of night.

Fred Sedgwick

Tracey's Tree

Wes Magee

A poem to read on the worst sort of day. This is, of course, another very difficult area. I found this poem invaluable when a similar tragedy happened in a school where I was, like Wes Magee, the headteacher. There are several technical points to which you could draw the children's attention: the repetition of the last line in each stanza, the run-on 'ran/across', the bluntness of the sentence: 'The lorry struck her.' Think about what has happened between the full stop after 'her' and the beginning of the next sentence: the immediate crisis, the realisation of how serious it is, the ambulance, the terrible news, the weeping, the announcement in assembly, the solemn talks with the child's parents, the funeral, the memorial service; all this takes place in the time it takes to read a full stop. There is a curious paradox here: technical examination of the poem intensifies the teacher's and children's sense of it, strengthens their grasp of it, while reducing the chances of distress. Ask the children: 'What are the raindrops in the poem for?'

Auntie Win

Peter Dixon

Children think about death. This poem gives them another opportunity to reflect on it. Notice another rhyme issue: this poem doesn't rhyme at all, until that evocative last word 'Psalms' is hammered home with the help of 'arms', itself preceded with the equally evocative word, given the context, 'empty'. The children might try to write a poem, with one rhyming pair, the second half of which is the last word in the poem. They might begin by simply making a list of objects that remind them of someone they love.

Some performance poems

We have already had a couple. This section is here more for fun in performance rather than as exemplars for writing. Fun teaches, though, and is not to be underrated in the classroom, especially with poetry. Also, performing a poem helps in the process of making it ours, and it also helps to bring the poem closer to children's lives, and further from the dry page.

Be Merry
Traditional

The first time with this poem, read lines 1 and 2 in each stanza yourself in as mock-mournful a voice as possible, with the children supplying all the last lines as a chorus. Then reverse roles, getting the children to act their dismal lines.

The Hairy Toe
Traditional

I read this poem to children as dramatically as possible, descending to a whisper on the last repetition of *'Who's got my hairy toe?'* in stanza 3, and then yelling as loud as I dare the last line. Put the children into groups of four or five and ask them to produce ways of reading this poem. Suggest that they relish all the sound words: 'moan', 'groan', 'crying', 'creaked', 'cracked', 'growled', 'rumbled' and 'creak'.

Here is another performance poem:

John Randall

O where have you been to, John Randall my son?
O where have you been to, my sweet pretty man?
I've been to my sweetheart, Mother. Make my bed soon
For I'm weary with hunting, and fain would lie down.

What did she give you, John Randall my son?
What did she give you, my sweet pretty man?
Eels fried in a pan, Mother. Make my bed soon
For I'm weary with hunting, and fain would lie down.

What colour were they, John Randall my son?
What colour were they, my sweet pretty man?
All spickled and spackled, Mother. Make my bed soon
For I'm weary with hunting, and fain would lie down.

What became of your bloodhounds, John Randall my son?
What became of your bloodhounds, my sweet pretty man?
They swelled and they died, Mother. Make my bed soon
For I'm weary with hunting, and fain would lie down.

I fear you are poisoned, John Randall my son.
I fear you are poisoned, my sweet pretty man.
Yes, I am poisoned, Mother. Make my bed soon
For I'm weary with hunting, and fain would lie down.

What'll you leave your brother, John Randall my son?
What'll you leave your brother, my sweet pretty man?
My clothes and my jewels, Mother. Make my bed soon
For I'm weary with hunting, and fain would lie down.

What'll you leave your sweetheart, John Randall my son?
What'll you leave your sweetheart, my sweet pretty man?
A rope for to hang her. Make my bed soon
For I'm weary with hunting, and fain would lie down.

Traditional

It works as a kind of radio play for two voices. The part of 'Mother' should be read with mounting horror, and the part of 'John' with mounting bitterness.

To the Moon

Thomas Hardy

This poem can be usefully performed, as well. One child, or one group of children, reads the first three lines of each stanza, and another child or group, reads the last four. I have pointed out in notes to earlier poems how children should understand the tone of lines. Some useful discussion will develop from questions like: 'How does the moon's voice sound in this poem?' 'What sort of God does Hardy seem to believe in?'

The children should look for the alliteration in this poem. There are internal rhymes as well: rhymes that are not only in the last lines of each stanza. Look at the way Hardy uses the sound 'O'.

Ask the children to write a poem to any noble part of creation: a star, a planet, the sun. This writer has seen the structure of Hardy's poem, and imitated it:

To a Star

'Why do you twinkle in the darkened sky?
    Why?'
'My light is reflected from the sun,
    The stupid, silly, shining sun
        That keeps the earth so bright and lively
        And annoys me in my peace.'

'Why do you only come out at night,
    You beautiful shining star?'
'I only come out at night because
    The sun doesn't bother to shine on me
        When the earth turns a bright pinky light,
        That's all the sun's fault.'

'Why is the light in your heart dampened
    To hear about the sun and earth?'
'Terrible they are, with such beauty and joy
    Never think about me, a twinkling nightlight
        That brightens the darkest nights,
        If only they knew, if only they knew.'

Annie (10)
(Bealings Primary School, Hertfordshire)

A Man of Words
Traditional

This poem should be performed in a crescendo: that is, start quietly, then get increasingly loud and menacing, until the children are shouting 'you're dead, and dead, and dead indeed!'

Some useful discussion is to be had here. Is this poem about a false lover? A politician? Who else could it be?

Note the rhyme: exact rhyming couplets. Ask the children to count the syllables in each line. When children try rhyming couplets, they are insufficiently aware of the metre. Getting the syllable count right is a beginning – only a beginning – to solving the problem. Able children might like to know that each line is made up of four iambs: an unaccented syllable followed by an accented one:

a MAN of WORDS and NOT of DEEDS
is LIKE a GARden FULL of WEEDS...

Any reading of this poem should balance this metre with how the sense of the poem dictates. A reading only concentrating on the metre would be dull.

Prayer
Traditional

Ask children to speak this poem in a spooky voice, and then to write a chant or a curse to protect you at night, ending 'Good Lord deliver us'.

I Am

Peter Dixon

Ask the children to write an 'I am' poem: a cheerful one beginning:

I am the glint of light from a Christmas tree

Or one like Peter Dixon's:

I am the finger pinched in the door

Meet-on-the-Road

Traditional

Perform it! The first line in each stanza should be read with increasing menace, up to 'I wish the wind...'; the next stanza ('What are those bells ringing for?') begins with panic. The last stanza's first lines must be read with great haste. The child's voice should stay brave and strong, as a contrast to Meet-on-the-Road's varying, wicked emotions.

Ask the children: 'Who is Meet-on-the-Road?' The Devil? Perhaps. What other people threaten children today? This poem can lead to useful discussion in PSME about the dangers surrounding children. I don't think I have to be specific here.

What Are Heavy?

Christina Rossetti

This poem is another question poem (see 'Seven Wishes') but this time the poet supplies answers. It is not difficult to perform (one child asks the questions, the other supplies the answers) or to imitate:

What is hot? Blazing sun and anger.
What is cold? Snowflakes and sadness.
What is murky? The graveyard and fog.
What is windy? Blowy wind and snow.

a 10-year-old
(Radburn School, Hertfordshire)

I Remember

Thomas Hood

This poem is printed here partly in memory of my mother, who used to say it to me in a sing-song Irish accent. I began to feel superior to this poem as I grew up, and I thought it was sentimental. Now I appreciate it for what it is: beautiful and very, very sad. I say it to children, and ask them what the mood of it is. They usually pick up the sense of the lines at the end of the first and last stanzas. This is one of the easiest lessons to teach. I ask the children, in the blind silence brought about by the closing of their eyes, to think of three or four early memories.

One girl wrote these heart-breaking lines:

> I remember, I remember
> When my parents divorced.
> I was four.
> I got up in the morning as usual.
> My mum told me
> My dad wasn't coming back.
> I remember, I remember
> The sharp pain
> That hit me all over.
> The sour smell
> That made me sick.
> I felt alone
> As if no-one could ever touch me again.

It helps the children to write if you, the teacher, have prepared memories of your own. This has two good effects. The first is that it helps them to write, and the second is that it shows that, despite all appearances to the contrary, you are a human being. Here is a teacher's example:

> I remember
> my mother making me stand in a corner of a store
> one December in the fifties
> telling me not to look
> and on Christmas morning
> I found
> that she had bought me
> a fire engine with a bell that rang
> as I pushed it along.

Riddle

Traditional

Riddles are not easy to teach, for two reasons. First, when the children get answers wrong, it is often because they are focusing on a single element in the poem, rather than the whole poem. For example, on hearing 'I have ears' (from an unwritten riddle about corn), the children see 'head'. Most classes have to be shown that the answer to each riddle has to fit every line. Second, children often have an idea in their minds that a riddle is a joke along the lines of 'What sits in a chair and whistles?' and so on.

The teaching of riddles depends on reading (or reciting) as many riddles as possible as clearly as possible. It should go without saying that an enthusiasm on the part of the teacher for the language of riddles (which is, to a large extent, an enthusiasm for the language of poetry) is an indispensable condition for this work.

There are three rules for genuine poetry riddles. Like all rules, they are not unbreakable. But, again, like all rules, they help. They are as follows:

The answer to the riddle should speak the riddle. In other words, the poem should either begin 'I', have 'I' somewhere in the poem, or use the word 'my' or 'me'. See nearly all the riddles quoted below.

The riddle should almost certainly contain either a simile or a metaphor. The word 'like' is a help here: it leads to similes. After the children grasp this idea, they can usually move on to metaphor, where there is no 'like': the subject is simply described in terms of something else.

It is better that the riddle should be too difficult rather than too easy. Riddles about the sun should avoid the word 'shines', for example, and riddles about rivers usefully avoid the word 'flows'. Similarly, riddles about mirrors (a good subject) should avoid the word 'reflects'.

The poem is the main thing in the writer's mind. Here are some children's riddles, from Ashwell Primary School in Hertfordshire:

> I run steadily shaping myself differently wherever I go
> Over sharp and smooth never scratching myself
>   because I don't have skin.
> I babble even though I cannot speak, and gurgle
>   even though I have no mouth.
> I follow my path wherever it may go. Making
>   images of wherever I may be.
>
> [water]
> Rosie (10)

I am struck by the way the lines are long, like water in a river is. I had not suggested this. I am also struck by resonant words and phrases like 'steadily shaping myself differently' (it is hard to believe that this writer had no idea of the word 'protean'), 'babble', 'gurgle' and 'making images'. I felt when I read this (the first riddle completed in this session, done in about fifteen minutes) that the request to make the poem 'difficult' had paid off.

Nobody could guess the answer to the next riddle. Children suggested 'gun' at first, then 'bomb' and so on. This piece was written out at first in prose, and the final repetition of the recurring phrase 'killing machine' – the last line – was added at my suggestion. Note the amazing puns on 'roll' and 'strike':

I am a killing machine.
I roll around.
I am a killing machine
killing everyone
who falls into my trap
everyday.
I strike and kill.
I am a killing machine.
They think I am cool
and I like that
because they fall in my trap
like that.
They sell me in stores
and I like that too.
I am a killing machine.

[cigarette]
Anon. (10)

I helped this writer to make his poem into short lines. But the satire was all his own.

I'm with you, always.
You wear me out each day.
You ignore me, always
as if I'm not really there.
I'm ugly but I'm pretty.
I'm kind but I'm mean.
I help you always
and you never, ever say thank you.

[life]
Zena

Here is one last riddle:

It is greater than God,
More evil than the devil.
Poor men have lots of it,
Rich men have none of it.
If you eat it you die.

[Nothing]

The last half of each line, of course, applies to the first half of the next: 'with a fiery tail I saw a comet. Drop down hail I saw a cloud...' and so on. Much as cathedrals remind us of worshippers who have prayed in centuries before us, little verses like this remind us that the human race has always had a sense of humour, and that human beings have always gone to considerable lengths to make jokes.

I Saw

Traditional

Now the Hungry Lion Roars

William Shakespeare

Here is some approachable Shakespeare. Ask the children to write a poem with the repeating line 'Now it is the time of night'.

Here is a poem from a school in Enfield:

Now it is the time of night
I hear people laughing outside my house
Now it is the time of night
I hear people throwing bottles when they've finished with them.
Now it is the time of night
I hear drunk people...

At this point in the play – at the beginning of Act 5 – Puck, the speaker of these lines, is beginning to close things down. Children could be asked to prepare ways of saying the lines in various moods or tones: bitterly, exhausted, menacingly...

Goodnight

Thomas Hood

Ask the children to write a goodnight poem for their grandparents, or their baby sisters and brothers, or for themselves.

Psalm 23	The Bible
God be in my head	Anon
Lord of all Gardens	Fred Sedgwick

I offer few notes for the last four poems in my book, apart from these words. Children should have Psalm 23 in what Philip Larkin called their 'myth-kitty'. They are the poorer if they do not. 'God be in my head' is both simple and profound. I remember how it moved me as a child when we sang it at primary school. I hope my poem/song for my goddaughter offers a chance for children to reflect and perhaps sing.

Will There Really Be a 'Morning'?

Emily Dickinson

Emily Dickinson welcomed us with flowers and stars at the beginning of this book, and here she is again at the close; 'a little Pilgrim', like the children we teach and, if we are wise, like ourselves.